CU00692846

Let Us Be Loved

Elizabeth of the Trinity

EUGENE McCAFFREY OCD

First published 2008 by:

TERESIAN PRESS
Carmelite Priory
Boars Hill
Oxford OX1 5HB
priory@carmelite.org.uk

Copyright © Eugene McCaffrey, OCD 2008

ISBN 978-0-947916-08-4

Cover illustration: photograph of Elizabeth, aged 13,
in commemoration of her First Prize at the Piano, July 24th, 1893
(picture taken beginning of August 1893);
reproduced by kind permission of the Carmelite Sisters of Dijon

Cover design by Bill Bolger

Typeset and printed by Joshua Horgan, Oxford

To all my sisters and brothers in Carmel,
companions along the way

Contents

Foreword

It is a great pleasure for me to introduce the Teresian Press, publications of the Anglo-Irish Province of the Teresian, or 'Discalced', Carmelites. While the Press has brought out a number of books and booklets over the past few years – including the Carmelite missal and breviary – I would now like to introduce a new series of works, the aim of which is to popularise and promote Carmelite spirituality and the life of prayer.

It is fitting that the first title in our new series is *Let Yourself Be Loved* by Fr Eugene McCaffrey, OCD. He himself is a gifted and experienced teacher of prayer, and his book is devoted to Elizabeth of the Trinity whose centenary has just been celebrated in the Order and throughout the world. Future publications include prayerful reflections on Scripture, the teachings of our saints, firsthand accounts of the experience of prayer, and the personal impact of Carmel.

Thomas Merton, in *The Ascent to Truth*, paid this striking tribute to our Order: 'There is no member of the Church,' he wrote, 'who does not owe something to Carmel.' My hope is that the work of the Teresian Press will, in some small way, continue that contribution to the Church and enrich its readers with the teachings and witness of our Carmelite saints and our authors today.

John Grennan, OCD
Provincial, Anglo-Irish Province

Preface

November 9th, 2006 marked a hundred years since the death of Elizabeth of the Trinity. The centenary year itself was a grace-filled invitation to reflect more deeply on the life and message of this exceptional woman – young, talented, a gifted musician, with a great joy for living and a hunger for prayer and for God: *'God in me, I in him', oh! that is my life!* (L 62).[1] Every aspect of her life and spirituality revolves around this major theme.

The renowned theologian Hans Urs von Balthasar spoke of Elizabeth of the Trinity and Thérèse of Lisieux as representing two 'hemispheres' that together give the totality and beauty of Carmelite spirituality.[2] However, while Thérèse erupted in a storm of glory, Elizabeth, humanly speaking, had to bide her time: it was over seventy years after her death before the publication of her complete works, and another four before she was raised to the altar.

Now, for her, the fullness of time has come. And she speaks a message of great urgency and importance for the Church of the new millennium. Her 'coming of age' also coincides with, and is in some way linked to, a rediscovery of the essential place of the mystery of the Trinity in Christian life. Theologians today present the Trinity, not as an idea or a concept to baffle and impress us, but as an invitation to enter into a communion of love and friendship with a God who loves us without limits. At the same time, this dynamic of invitation and friendship is very much part of the global search for better relationships between peoples and nations, where concepts such as unity and diversity, person and relationship, are the key to peace and reconciliation.

Elizabeth saw all human life flowing from and returning to the Trinity. She did not see a 'mystery' but a Lover, a Friend, a Companion – a real community of persons with whom she could share her life. For her, God was a God who was faithful and who, she often felt, loved her *too* much! This was what she called her 'secret', a secret she is now called upon to proclaim in our day: that God is not just loving but loves us 'to excess'. This phrase, she claimed, could be taken as a summary of her whole life (cf. L 280; Eph 2:4).

Elizabeth of the Trinity – the child with fire in her eyes, the virtuoso pianist with rhythm in her head, the teenager who loved glamorous hats and lived life to the full, the lay contemplative in a world of travel, parties and dance, the nun wrapped in silence, the lover of Christ pouring out her life for the Church and for the world – is for us a beacon of light, a prophet of the presence of God, a praise of glory, and most of all *a brilliant witness to the joy of being rooted and grounded in love.*[3]

In the centenary year that has just ended, many new publications have appeared: books, articles, critical studies, DVDs. There were also lecture series, seminars and symposiums – not only within the Carmelite family, but throughout the Christian world as a whole. It seemed as if the Spirit was speaking directly through her life and writings and offering a message of hope and encouragement to the modern world as it entered a new millennium.

The pages that follow are one small effort to introduce the life of Elizabeth to those seeking to know the secret of her spirituality and the richness of her teaching. They were originally written as a series of six leaflets – loose, easy to read, and presented as part of the general literature of the centenary year. But leaflets have a mind of their own and, like holy pictures, often turn up in the most unusual places!

It is fortuitous, then, that a new series of publications from the Teresian Press is being launched at this time, to popularise and promote Carmelite spirituality. I feel privileged that the first book chosen for the new series should be *Let Yourself Be Loved.* All the leaflets have been collated, though the overall text has been expanded for publication in book form. Among these changes, one new chapter has been added, to include some reflection on Elizabeth's musical talent, which more and more is being seen as central to her spirituality and to her expression of it.

Elizabeth's life was short – she died at the age of twenty-six – but her influence extends far beyond the limits of her earthly journey. She speaks a message greater than her span of years. Her young, sensitive heart intuited something often hidden from the wise and the clever and revealed only to little ones – she was aware of how greatly she was loved: *when I look back I see a divine pursuit of my soul; oh! what love, as if I were crushed beneath its weight* (L 151). It was this love that sustained her in her early struggle with her own turbulent nature, in her faithfulness to her vocation during her teenage years, in the dark night of her first years in Carmel, and in the final agony of trust and surrender as she journeyed into 'Light, Love, Life'. And it is this same love that transfigures all her writings – the secret she longs to share with every restless heart searching for meaning and for love: *I would like to whisper this secret to those I love so they too might always cling to God through everything* (L 122).

'Let yourself be loved' is not a cliché or a pious catchphrase. It is a way of life, an unfailing password into the heart of God.

I would like to express my sincere thanks to all who have helped in any way to make this book possible. I am especially grateful to my colleague Jennifer Holden, of the Tabor retreat team, Preston, for the time and effort she gave to the original publication of the centenary leaflets; to Joanne Mosley for her continuing support and encouragement; and to the Carmelite Sisters of Dijon for their kind permission to use the photographs of Elizabeth of the Trinity.

A Woman for Our Times

*It seems to me that I have found
my Heaven on earth,
since Heaven is God,
and God is [in] my soul.
The day I understood that,
everything became clear to me.
I would like to whisper this secret
to those I love so they too
might always cling to God
through everything.*
(L 122)

A Centenary

November 9th, 2006 marked the centenary of the death of Blessed Elizabeth of the Trinity. Her life and teaching have had a profound influence on the Church's spirituality over the past hundred years. Pope John Paul II referred to her as one of the great spiritual writers of the twentieth century and openly acknowledged her influence on his own life. She has been called a *prophet of the presence of God*,[4] a living witness to the reality of God's creative and dynamic presence in our lives and in the world.

During her centenary year – from the feast of the Trinity 2006 to Trinity Sunday 2007 – the Church, and in particular the Carmelite family, celebrated her life and teaching, reflecting together on the relevance of her message to a world still hungry for a deeper meaning to life and for the spiritual values of the gospel.

This book is offered as an introduction to Elizabeth's life and spirituality, and as an invitation to explore still further the rich depths of her own writings.

Early Life

Elizabeth Catez was born at the military camp of Avor, near Bourges, France, on July 18th, 1880 where her father, an army officer, was stationed. Two years later, he was transferred to Dijon where a second daughter, Marguerite, was born in 1883. Elizabeth was a lively, energetic child with a volatile and tempestuous nature as formidable as a cavalry charge!

When Elizabeth was seven years old, her father suffered a fatal heart attack and her mother and the two daughters moved to a modest house in

the town, close to the Carmelite convent. Elizabeth gradually learnt to overcome her tantrums and 'tears of rage'. She was a bright, intelligent girl – known affectionately as 'Sabeth' – full of natural charm and spontaneous gaiety. She made friends easily and entered fully into the social life of Dijon. She loved music and dancing, was fond of hiking and travel and, at the same time, was sensitive to the beauty both of nature and of art. Musically, she was very gifted and studied at the Conservatory in Dijon where she won many prizes for her piano-playing.

An Open Heart

But a deeper love soon began to show itself in this young girl of generous and upright heart. From her teenage years, she was deeply touched by the love of God and inspired by the life and story of Jesus as portrayed in the gospel. She felt a personal call to prayer and became more and more aware of God's presence in her life and in the hidden depths of her soul. At the age of fourteen she consecrated herself to God and began to think seriously of a vocation to the religious life. When she was seventeen she asked permission to enter the Carmelite convent, but in deference to her mother's wishes agreed to postpone this till after her twenty-first birthday.

For the next few years Elizabeth gave much of her time to social and pastoral work, running a youth club for working-class children and teaching catechism. She became a *contemplative in the world*, quietly witnessing to the presence and power of God in her own life and in that of the people with whom she mixed. When she was twenty a Dominican priest, Fr Vallée, explained to her the doctrine of the *indwelling* – the mystery of God's personal presence in the human heart – and this, together with her own experience in prayer, opened for her a way of interior prayer that was to characterise her short life.

In Carmel

After many obstacles, Elizabeth entered the Carmelite convent of Dijon in August 1901 at the age of twenty-one. Here she felt completely at home, and for the next five years her life in the convent was indistinguishable from that of the other sisters apart from the unseen workings of grace and the action of the Spirit in her heart. She made her religious profession in January 1903 and gave herself unreservedly to a hidden life of prayer and sacrifice in the service of the Church and the world. Her name, 'Elizabeth', meaning 'House of God',[5] became a summary of her life of praise, sacrifice and love: *I am 'Elizabeth of the Trinity',* she said, *that is, Elizabeth disappearing, losing herself, letting herself be invaded by the Three* (L 172).

Within the cloistered walls of the Carmelite convent, the deep graces of interior prayer she experienced as a lay contemplative flowered and matured. Through faith, Elizabeth lived in an ever-deepening relationship of love with the Trinity within her soul. In November 1904, she composed her beautiful *Prayer to the Trinity* – one of the best-known and best-loved prayers of contemporary spirituality, which has even made its way into the Church's *Catechism* (# 260). It is a bold and audacious plea that she might become another incarnation of the Word, so that in her he might renew his whole mystery. At the same time, she discovered the writings of St Paul and found in them the inspiration and assurance she needed to fulfil what she so longed to be: a *Praise of Glory* of the Trinity:

A praise of glory is a soul of silence
that remains like a lyre
under the mysterious touch of the Holy Spirit
so that He may draw from it divine harmonies.
(HF 43)

In the spring of 1906, Elizabeth became seriously ill. Her condition grew rapidly worse and was to result in her death before the end of the year. *Before I die*, she wrote to a friend, *I dream of being transformed into Jesus Crucified* (L 324). Her dream became a reality during those last nine months of her life. Diagnosed with Addison's Disease, her frail body was ravaged with physical pain and exhaustion, and her spirit was plunged into darkness and aridity. One of her prayers, spoken only a few days before she died, captures the whole spirit of her life and death: *you know if I love you... Exhaust the whole of my substance for your glory. May it be distilled drop by drop for your Church.*[6] Her last words were: *I am going to Light, to Love, to Life!*[7] The process of canonisation was introduced in May 1931, and she was beatified on November 25th, 1984.

Selections from her writings were published shortly after her death. But these made up only a portion of the complete spiritual heritage left by Elizabeth. To mark the centenary of her birth in 1980, the complete works were published in three volumes, under the title *I Have Found*

God. They have now been translated into all major languages.[8]

Elizabeth's message and her invitation to follow it are as relevant today as when she herself expressed it:

> *Let us live with God as with a friend,*
> *let us make our faith a living faith*
> *in order to be in communion with*
> *Him through everything,*
> *for that is what makes saints.*
> *We possess our Heaven within us,*
> *since He who satisfies the hunger*
> *of the glorified in the light of vision*
> *gives Himself to us in faith and mystery,*
> *it is the Same One!*
> (L 122)

From Her Writings

> *It is there, right in the depths,*
> *in the Heaven of my soul,*
> *that I love to find Him since He never leaves me.*
> *'God in me, I in him', oh! that is my life!...*
> *Have I ever told you what my name in Carmel will be:*
> *'Marie-Elizabeth of the Trinity'.*
> *It seems to me that this name indicates*
> *a special vocation;*
> *isn't it beautiful?*
> (L 62)

For my heart is always with Him,
And night and day it thinks unceasingly
Of this heavenly and divine Friend
To whom it would like to prove its affection.
(P 43)

Let us love Him,
let us live with Him as with a loved one
from whom we cannot be separated.
(L 280)

Prophet of the Presence of God

*I leave you my faith
in the presence of God,
of the God who is all Love
dwelling in our souls.
I confide to you:
it is this intimacy with Him 'within'
that has been the beautiful sun
illuminating my life, making it already
an anticipated Heaven.*
(L 333)

Remain in My Love

The message of Elizabeth of the Trinity *is spreading today*, John Paul II has declared, *with a prophetic force*.[9] She is a prophet in the sense of someone who reminds us of a forgotten truth, sheds new light on old mysteries and stands out as a sure and steady guide in a world of uncertainty and ambiguity. Her life has become a beacon of light for us, a call to discover once again the truth that God not only loves each one of us personally but is also intimately and uniquely present to us.

The presence of which Elizabeth speaks is not a vague, indiscriminate power but something personal and individual. God is not the *ground of our being* in some dry, remote sort of way. We are not *surrounded* by God as by air, light or energy: he is a *personal* God who knows each of us individually and cares for us uniquely.
Yet God is not just present *to* us, no matter how personal and immediate that may be; he is also present *within* us.

This is the great truth of which Jesus spoke at the Last Supper: *those who love me will...win my Father's love and we will come and make our home in them* (Jn 14:23). It is an *indwelling* presence; a *homing* presence, through which God is at home in the human heart; a presence based on choice, love and friendship.

I am asking the Holy Spirit to show you this presence of God within you, Elizabeth writes to her mother, adding, *...if you read the Gospel of John, you will see...that the Master insists on this commandment: 'Remain in me, and I in you'* (L 273). She was conscious, not only of the gospel teaching, but also of the great Carmelite tradition she had inherited, inspired by the example and

24

words of the prophet Elijah, who *lived in the presence of God* (cf. 1Kgs 17:1).

'Little Bethany'

The writings of Elizabeth of the Trinity offer a fresh insight into the gospels and are an inspiration and encouragement for all who struggle along the way of the spirit. Her writings are not scholarly or systematic: they are a reflection of her own experience in prayer and of her ever-deepening awareness of the reality and power of God in her life.

The doctrine of the indwelling became the key to her own spiritual life and is central to her teaching. She wished to *live through love in his presence* (Eph 1:4); her life was essentially a response to this presence, an awareness of the One dwelling in the depths of her heart. She wanted more than anything else to retire within herself and live in the little *cell* – the *little Bethany*, she called it (IN 5) – which God had built in her heart. *I have found my Heaven on earth*, she wrote, *since Heaven is God, and God is [in] my soul* (L 122).

A Lay Contemplative

Once, when Elizabeth was unable to attend Mass because of illness, she wrote to her friend Canon Isidore Angles: *I am prevented from*

going to church, from receiving
holy communion but, you
see, God has no need of the
sacrament to come to me, it
seems to me that I have Him
just as much; it is so good,
this presence of God! (L 62).

Elizabeth was able to find the fullness of God's presence everywhere and in everything, through an ongoing awareness of his dwelling within her: *It is there, right in the depths, in the Heaven of my soul, that I love to find Him since He never leaves me. 'God in me, I in him', oh! that is my life!* (L 62).

These words were written while Elizabeth was still a young woman living in Dijon, where she was actively involved in youth work, teaching catechism and visiting the sick and elderly. Few could have guessed at the depths of spiritual longing hidden within the heart of this young woman. Awareness of God's presence was a formative part of her everyday experience – an attitude, an approach to life, quietly nourishing her and shaping her outlook and decisions.

The summer months of travel with her family and friends were filled with tennis, croquet, musical sessions and a constant round of parties. Elizabeth, always lively and endowed with great charm, was fully part of this social scene. But already there was an air of mystery about her;

she was someone aware of a deeper voice echoing within. At a dance, someone was heard to remark, 'She's not for us, look at her expression.'[10] Her dancing partners read her well. Elizabeth was listening to a different music; her heart was already captive to a greater and deeper call.

His Presence, My Joy

At the heart of Elizabeth's teaching is the need for stillness and silence, a silence of listening and openness to the *still, small voice* of the Spirit within. In an age of ever-increasing noise and activity, her teaching shines like a beacon of sanity and carries a message of hope. It is the message of God's love, of his presence in our lives, and of his invitation to intimacy. Most important of all, Elizabeth speaks out of her own experience, out of the lived reality of her own life. A young woman rich in human qualities, vibrant with the sensitivity of an artist and the courage of a soldier, she speaks words of wisdom and of common sense.

Once Elizabeth discovered, at the age of ten, that her name meant *House of God*,[11] she was determined to make that house a home, where she would live as attentively as possible to the presence within. This presence became her joy. Though she lived only twenty-six years, it was enough for her to live with total intensity, both as a lay contemplative and as a Carmelite nun, the mystery of God's life that she shared through baptism. To an age searching for meaning and identity, she tells of her own search and her own discovery: her thirst for the deeper reality within and the joy of finding, and surrendering to, love: *love is something infinite*, she once wrote, *and you can always go farther in infinity!* (L 192).

Prophet of the presence of God, Elizabeth invites us to accept this *gift of God* and open our hearts to the reality within:

> *He is always there,*
> *although you don't feel it;*
> *He is waiting for you*
> *and wants to establish*
> *a 'wonderful communion' with you.*
> (L 249)

From Her Writings

> *Love...dwells within us;*
> *and my only exercise*
> *is to enter within once again,*
> *to lose myself*
> *in Those who are there!*
> (L 179)

I am asking God to give you a taste, too,
of the sweetness of His Love and His presence:

that is what transforms, what illumines life,
it is the secret of happiness!
(L 174)

In that little inner sanctuary [of my soul],
…I find Him at every hour
of the day and night.
I'm never alone:
my Christ is always there
praying in me,
and I pray with Him.
(L 123)

Mary, Gate of Heaven

In what peace, in what recollection
Mary lent herself to everything she did!
How even the most trivial things
were divinized by her!
For through it all the Virgin remained
the adorer of the gift of God!
This did not prevent her
from spending herself outwardly
when it was a matter of charity.
(HF 40)

Gate of Heaven

Elizabeth of the Trinity loved to refer to the Blessed Virgin as the *Gate of Heaven*, the name she had given to a statue of Our Lady of Lourdes which she had with her in the Dijon Carmel. The title resonated with her own name and spirituality: 'Elizabeth', *House of God* – her own soul, in which God dwelt as in a home. Elizabeth saw Mary standing at the threshold of her heart, opening a way into the mysterious place of the indwelling of God.

At the age of fourteen, Elizabeth dedicated her life to God and placed her resolution and her whole self in the hands of the Blessed Virgin. She wrote, around this time, her first known poem:

> *Mary, O tender Mother,*
> *I place myself under your protection.*
> *Listen to my prayer*
> *And bless my resolutions.*
> (P 1)

Five years later, she wrote in her diary: *On each feast of Mary, I renew my consecration to this good Mother. So today I entrusted myself to her, and once again threw myself into her arms. With the utmost confidence, I recommended to her my future, my vocation* (D 2). During a visit to Lourdes, Elizabeth renewed her commitment and entrusted all her hopes and longings to Mary. She wished to offer her life for the Church and the world – an offering constantly renewed and fully lived out in all its starkness within the hidden, silent world of the Carmelite cloister.

Echo of God

As a Carmelite, Elizabeth was very conscious of Mary's presence in her life: *Ask the Queen of Carmel, our Mother, to teach you to adore Jesus in profound recollection; she so loves her daughters in Carmel, her privileged order, and she is our foremost patron* (L 136).

Just as Jesus found his home in the womb of Mary, so Elizabeth found in that same womb a place of encounter and intimacy with God: *I delight in her beauty*, writes Elizabeth, *like a child who loves its mother*; and she adds confidently, *I feel strongly drawn to her, I've made her Queen and Guardian of my heaven* (L 298). It was close to the heart of Mary that she learned to listen in deepest silence and stillness to the Word of God within. Just as Elizabeth called her own sister Guite the *echo of my soul* (L 204),[12] in the same way she would have understood Mary as an 'echo of the heart of God'.

Praise of Glory

Elizabeth was inspired by the writings of St Paul: her *dear saint* (L 306), she called him, whose writings were *so simple and at the same time so profound* (L 250). She especially identified with a phrase used by Paul: *Before the world was made, God chose us in Christ…so that we might become the praise of glory of his grace* (Eph 1:4.6).

Jesus, the exact likeness of the Father, is the perfect praise of his glory. And Mary, his mother, is the faithful echo of that same praise, as we hear

Carmel of Dijon

in her exultant song of joy, the *Magnificat*. Elizabeth longed to enter into that song of praise and adoration. Towards the end of her life she even signed some of her letters with the name, *Praise of Glory*. She writes: *I am going to tell you a very personal secret: my dream is to be 'the praise of His glory', I read that in Saint Paul and [Jesus] made me understand that this was to be my vocation while in exile, waiting to go [to] sing the eternal Sanctus in the City of the saints* (L 256). But Elizabeth knew that no one had penetrated the mystery of Christ in all its depth as had the Blessed Virgin. *This Mother of grace will form my soul so that her little child will be a living, 'striking' image of her first-born, the Son of the Eternal, He who was the perfect praise of His Father's glory* (LR 2).

Mother of Souls

Elizabeth saw Mary as mother, friend, companion and sister.

She longed, like Mary, to become a *spiritual mother*, bringing forth children for God – brothers and sisters of Christ; her prayer was that she would *be fruitful, a co-redemptress, bring forth souls to grace* (IN 13). She found in Mary an example

33

of faithfulness and openness to the activity of the Spirit. *It seems to me that the attitude of the Virgin during the months that elapsed between the Annunciation and the Nativity is the model for interior souls, those whom God has chosen to live within* (HF 40).

But no matter how much Elizabeth longed to be an apostle and harvester for Christ, she knew this was essentially a work of grace and the fruit of prayer. Her contemplative gaze penetrated to the heart of human reality, and her silent prayer embraced the world in love and compassion. The only one who has any impact in the world of grace is the one who, like Mary, is united to the heart of Christ. *The Carmelite...has found the One Thing Necessary, the divine Being, Light and Love. When she envelops the world in her prayer, she is truly an apostle* (P 83).

Apostle and Carmelite

Elizabeth saw Mary as the realisation and fulfilment of her own vocation – an ideal just as relevant to the lay contemplative. *'The Virgin kept all these things in her heart': her whole history can be summed up in these few words! It was within her heart that she lived* (LR 40).

For Elizabeth, Mary was the measure of her striving, a faithful companion on the way, a sister in whom she could confide and find encouragement

Statue of Mary – Dijon Carmel

and support. *I...unite myself to the soul of the Virgin at the time when the Father was overshadowing her, while the Word was becoming incarnate within her, and the Holy Spirit was coming upon her to bring about the great mystery* (L 246). Elizabeth understood Mary's mission as being not only to lead us to her Son, but also to help transform us into his image and likeness. This is a vocation in which she longed to share: like Mary, to bring forth other Christs to enrich the Church and give glory to the Father. *'Apostle, Carmelite'*, she wrote to a missionary friend, *it is all one!* (L 124).

Behold Your Mother

As her health failed and the shadow of suffering spread across her frail body, Elizabeth discovered in a new way the Virgin standing at the foot of the cross: *now that [Jesus] has returned to the Father and has substituted me for Himself on the Cross...the Blessed Virgin is again there to teach me to suffer as He did* (LR 41). And she comments: *This Queen of virgins is also Queen of martyrs; but again it was in her heart that the sword pierced, for with her everything took place within!* (LR 41). In sharing the sufferings of Christ, Elizabeth could find no finer example than the strong, heroic woman standing at the foot of the cross: *She is there at the foot of the Cross, standing, full of strength and courage, and here my Master says to me: 'Behold your Mother.' He gives her to me for my Mother* (cf. LR 41).

At the Foot of the Cross

During the last year of her life Elizabeth was called to enter, in a special way, into the mystery of the cross. Here, more than ever, she turned to Mary, her *Gate of Heaven*. She had often pondered on Mary's role as co-redemptress, the woman specially chosen to share in the redemptive work of her Son. This was a role Elizabeth now felt drawn to share in an even deeper way than before. She understood that her desire to be transformed into Christ meant ultimately to be transformed into his death: *A Carmelite...is a soul who has gazed on the Crucified, who has seen Him offering Himself to His Father...and has wanted to give herself as He did!* (L 133).

In wishing to unite her sufferings with those of Christ and to share in his passion, Elizabeth was joining Mary in her faithful, silent witness at the foot of the cross: *the Blessed Virgin is again there...to make me hear those last songs of His soul which no one else but she, His Mother, could overhear* (LR 41).

From Her Writings

Take refuge in a Mother's heart,
the heart of the Virgin.
It knew all the breaking, all the tearing,
and it always stayed so calm, so strong,
for it always stayed leaning
on the heart of her Christ!
(L 134)

Think what must have been in the soul of the Virgin
when, after the Incarnation,
she possessed within her
the Incarnate Word, the Gift of God…
In what silence, what recollection,
what adoration she must have been wrapped
in the depth of her soul
in order to embrace this God
whose Mother she was.
(L 183)

A Girl with Rhythm in Her Head

In the light of faith,
may [we] go even now to sing,
with the blessed,
the hymn of love that is sung eternally
before the throne of the Lamb.
(L 194)

Language of the Heart

At one stage, Elizabeth took lessons in English, but without much success. She called it 'the language of the birds', which anyone who has listened to a dawn chorus may see as a compliment! Elizabeth was not good at languages or grammar, not even French: her education was restricted, her vocabulary limited, and her spelling erratic. Her language was that of the heart, a language that expressed itself in poetry, music and prayer.

For Elizabeth, the essential form of communication was through music; this was the language she spoke best. She was a gifted pianist with an intense love for music, a passion that was evident even from her earliest years.

At the age of eight she enrolled at the Dijon Conservatory of Music and quickly mastered even the most difficult skills and techniques. The piano became her daily universe. She often spent four or five hours a day practising, demonstrating a commitment and dedication rare in one so young. From an early age, Elizabeth began to play at public concerts. She won many prizes for piano-playing, including First Prize at the Dijon Conservatory when she was just thirteen. Even at such a young age, it was said of her that 'no one could interpret Chopin like her.'[13] She obviously had a great future ahead of her if she wished to pursue it. But Elizabeth had other thoughts: already she was tuning into a different voice and a deeper kind of music.

'I used to love speaking to him that way'[14]

For Elizabeth, the piano was a place where she met God. Music was, for her, a form of prayer: *When I can no longer pray, I play,* she told a friend.[15] She once said that she played her piano as if Jesus were the only one who could hear her. There was something in the way she played that came from the depth of her soul and found expression particularly in music. Her friends loved to listen to her playing: 'You felt that her whole body was moved by her soul...as though guided by some inner music.'[16] A virtuoso pianist, she was able to express the feelings of her heart in the power of a rhapsody, the grace of a waltz or the fervour of an Ave Maria. Her profound gift of spiritual listening owes a lot to the long hours spent at the keyboard. She listened to the music echoing within and captivating her young heart.

Elizabeth and her sister Guite

There is nothing so much like music as prayer. Elizabeth was captivated by both: music and prayer interwoven as an integral part of her spiritual journey. Music had a huge impact on the way she lived, the way she related to others, and on the way she prayed. She may have left her piano behind when she entered the convent but not her musician's heart. Her response to God in prayer was as focused and committed as was her dedication to the piano. Both were part of her journey; the music of the keyboard gave way to the silent music of the heart. The teenage girl with 'rhythm in her head' was also described by one of her friends as a 'soul full of harmonies'.[17]

Music of the Night

Once she entered the convent, there is no evidence that Elizabeth ever played the piano again. It was an offering made willingly: *I have never thought of anything but Carmel, she said, and I will gladly make the sacrifice of my piano. I feel I am made for the interior life.*[18] Despite her generosity, her first eighteen months in Carmel were by no means easy. At the beginning of her formation she entered into a period of great emotional, psychological and spiritual turmoil. Almost overnight she moved from the close, intimate network of family and friends to the austere, structured atmosphere of the convent. Her beautiful hats and dresses were replaced by the dull material of a postulant's garb and by the dark brown habit of Carmel. She must have felt the lack of emotional outlet that the piano had always given her. The whole social structure was so radically different: the parties, outings, the excitement of youth work were all replaced by a fixed community timetable and the strict routine of convent life.

Elizabeth entered into this dark and painful period for which she found very little redress. Yet it was a precious time, a time of purification, cleansing and spiritual growth. She suffered from scruples, over-anxiety and hypersensitivity. She had to learn to let go of her own plans and her own desires and move at God's pace, not her own. The hours of steadfast discipline and faithful practice at the piano must have stood her in good stead in those months of darkness and aridity. Music is the language of the heart, especially a heart that is in pain. It is also the evocative art form most closely associated with memory, memories often deeply felt but not always easy to express. Music is not just an escape; it is a way of coping. Even before she entered the convent, silence was part of Elizabeth's spiritual landscape. She knew how to listen with the ear of the heart. One of the awards she received at the Conservatory was for musical comprehension, the ability to listen to and discern musical patterns. She now listened to and discerned the movement of her own heart, the silence within and the deeper vibrations of the spirit. We sometimes forget just how crucial this was for Elizabeth, how much her musical soul must have found strength and solace in the established pattern of spiritual listening and openness: *I want to spend my life in listening to You,* she exclaimed in her great *Prayer to the Trinity.*

The Other Side of Silence

When words fail, music begins; when music ends, silence takes over. Silence is a fabric around which music is woven. And yet, sometimes, silence of itself is not enough. There is something deeper still, on the other side of silence. No one knew this better than Elizabeth. The search for what she called the 'unfathomable mystery' (P 91) was a constant motif in her life and a recurring theme in all her writings.

Elizabeth often described the spiritual life in musical terms: the positive aspects as harmonies, choruses and canticles; the negative ones as notes that were false, untrue or discordant. Yet she knew what every true artist knows: that it is the pause between the notes that makes the difference, the silence that is just as powerful and significant as the sound. She spoke of the lyre, so beloved by the psalmist, as a beautiful symbol of music that resonates in the soul and can best express the beauty and richness of the spiritual journey: *the Holy Spirit will transform you into a mysterious lyre, which, in silence, beneath His divine touch, will produce a magnificent canticle to Love* (L 269).

But in the end, for Elizabeth, it was love that mattered. Words, music, silence were all of a piece: love in search of fulfilment – love searching for Love. This was the one and only reality for which she ultimately longed. She understood that communion is the best form of communication. Prayer, in all its various phases – adoration, praise, thanksgiving and petition – is, ultimately, nothing other than a way of communing with 'a Being who is Love' (L 327).

From Her Writings

A praise of glory is a soul of silence
that remains like a lyre
under the mysterious touch
of the Holy Spirit
so that He may draw from it divine harmonies.
(HF 43)

A soul that debates with its self,
that is taken up with its feelings,
and pursues useless thoughts and desires,
scatters its forces,
for it is not wholly directed toward God.
Its lyre does not vibrate in unison
and when the Master plays it,
He cannot draw from it divine harmonies,
for it is still too human and discordant...
Instead of persevering in praise through
everything in simplicity,
it must continually adjust the strings
of its instrument
which are all a little out of tune.
(LR 3)

'My soul is always in my hands.'
My Master sang this in His soul,
and that is why in the midst of all His anguish
He always remained the calm and strong One.
(LR 3)

The Blessed Virgin is again there
[at the foot of the Cross]
to teach me to suffer as He did,
to tell me, to make me hear
those last songs of His soul
which no one else but she, His Mother,
could overhear.
(LR 41)

I listened to my Word whom I adore
And I heard the song that is sung
In the bosom of the Divinity.
(P 86)

God is Love

O my God, Trinity whom I adore,
help me to forget myself entirely
that I may be established in You
as still and as peaceful
as if my soul were already in eternity.
May nothing trouble my peace
or make me leave You,
O my Unchanging One.
(PT)

Baptised in Christ

St John of the Cross, we are told, loved to say a votive Mass of the Trinity. One day, when asked why this feast was so special to him, he replied with a gentle smile, 'because the Trinity is the greatest saint in heaven!' Elizabeth of the Trinity would have been delighted with his response. In fact, she said much the same herself: *this feast of the Three is really my own, for me there is no other like it* (L 113).

Elizabeth's special grace seems to have been an awareness of the indwelling of the Trinity in her own heart and in the hearts of all the baptised. It is central to her teaching and percolates through all her writings. This grace, she understood, is rooted in Christian baptism, by which we each become a *temple of the Holy Trinity* (L 197). Reflecting on the 'better part' chosen by Mary, the sister of Martha, in Luke's gospel, she wrote to a widow worrying about one of her daughters: *This better part, which seems to be my privilege in…Carmel, is offered by God to every baptized soul. He offers it to you, dear Madame, in the midst of your cares and maternal concerns. Believe that His whole desire is to lead you ever deeper into Himself* (L 129).

By baptism we are called to enter into a deep and personal relationship with God: we become beloved daughters and sons of the Father, brothers and sisters 'in Christ', and the dwelling place of the Holy Spirit. To her own married sister Elizabeth wrote: *I have just been reading in Saint Paul some splendid things on the mystery of the divine adoption. Naturally, I thought of you – it would have been quite extraordinary if I hadn't, for you are a mother and know what depths of love God has placed in your heart for your children, so you can grasp the grandeur of this mystery: to be children of God* (L 239).

Called by Name

Elizabeth did not speak of the Trinity in a logical or systematic way. She was not a theologian in the strict sense of the word; rather, she was a theologian of *experience* – a witness to the inner life of the soul. For her, the Trinity was not a dry, dogmatic statement or an abstract truth to be accepted just as an item of faith. It was something to  be *lived* and explored in the context of the 'good news' revealed in the pages of the gospel. Jesus himself never used the word 'Trinity' but spoke of the special love and relationship between the Father and the Son, who together would send the gift of the Spirit into the hearts of all who believe: a life-giving presence of friendship and love.

Before she entered Carmel, Elizabeth wanted to take the name 'Elizabeth of Jesus' but afterwards realised the significance of the name given to her. *Have I ever told you my name in Carmel?* she wrote to her friend Canon Angles. *...To me it seems that this name indicates a special vocation; isn't it a lovely name? I so love this mystery of the Holy Trinity, it is an abyss in which I lose myself!* (L 62). Her name added focus and direction to her life and her prayer: *my only exercise*, she told a friend, *is to enter within...to lose myself in Those who are there!* (L 179); *I am 'Elizabeth of the Trinity', that is, Elizabeth disappearing, losing herself, letting herself be invaded by the Three* (L 172).

The Greatness of His Love

For Elizabeth, God was not some lonely celibate dwelling in outer space, an absentee landlord remote from his own creation. Her understanding of God was simple and direct: *God is love* (1Jn 4:8.16). She quoted these words several times in her writings, sometimes placing them as a motto at the beginning of her letters.

Love, by definition, is relational; it is of the very nature of love to give and to share. This is how God has revealed himself in the Scriptures, especially in the luminous pages of the gospels: a God who *so loved the world that he gave his only Son...that we might have eternal life* (Jn 3:16). This is the only God Elizabeth knew: a passionate God, full of life, energy and love, personally and intimately involved in every aspect of our life and destiny.

Elizabeth was strongly drawn to Paul's words describing God as not just loving, but loving *to excess* (cf. Eph 2:4): *there is a phrase from Saint Paul that is like a summary of my life*, Elizabeth told her mother, *and could be written on every one of its moments: 'Because of His exceeding great love'* (cf. L 280). Elizabeth is a witness to the reality of this love; love is our true nature, it alone reveals who we are. We are called to live with God as with a *friend*, in the fellowship of love – a love that both gives and receives.

Trinity whom I Adore

On the feast of the Presentation of Mary, 1904, at the end of a community retreat, Elizabeth composed what is now known as her *Prayer to the Trinity*. Despite its brevity – fifty-three lines on one sheet of paper – it is one of the most inspirational spiritual documents of the twentieth century and, as we have seen, has even found its way into the *Catechism of the Catholic Church*. It was discovered untitled and unedited among her notes after her death, written in a bold, clear hand. It is not a statement or a treatise on prayer but a spontaneous explosion of a prayer-filled heart, an outburst of love that distils the essence of her spirituality. Like the priestly prayer of Jesus (Jn 17), we are drawn into an experience of prayer, privileged to overhear the deep outpouring of an enamoured heart. The prayer itself is a self-portrait, a synthesis of her life and spirituality.

Elizabeth was already familiar with the prayer of St Catherine of Siena, *O eternal Trinity*, which she had copied and kept among her books. She was even more familiar with Thérèse of Lisieux' *Offering to Merciful Love*, a prayer which Elizabeth copied several times and seems to have known practically by heart. She read *Story of a Soul* shortly after it was published and was profoundly influenced by Thérèse's spirituality. These two 'Sisters in the Spirit', as they have been called,[19] resonate with a similar understanding of God and with an awareness of his invitation to love.

My Three, My All

The prayer itself is contained in four paragraphs, the first and last addressed to the Trinity, the second – the longest – addressed to Christ, and the third to the Holy Spirit and the Father. A richness and variety of prayer is contained in each outpouring of the heart: petition, gratitude, surrender, adoration and praise, all overlapping and interlaced, as Elizabeth pleads passionately to be carried still further into the mystery of love.

She longs to love Christ – her *beloved Star* – even unto death, begging him to clothe her with himself, pleading that she may spend her life listening to him and never withdraw from his radiance. In an audacious plea, prompted by the folly of the saints, she begs the Holy Spirit to create

in her *a kind of incarnation of the Word* – that she may be *another humanity...in which He can renew His whole Mystery.* She entreats the Father to bend lovingly over her and to cover her with his shadow, so that he may see in her only the *Beloved in whom You are well pleased*. Her final plea to the *Three*, her *All*, is: *Bury Yourself in me that I may bury myself in You until I depart to contemplate in Your light the abyss of Your greatness.*

If it is true that prayer reflects who we are, then we are indeed privileged to penetrate, even if just a little, into the heart of Blessed Elizabeth: her *Prayer to the Trinity* both teaches and inspires us, reminding us of the greatness of our vocation and the everlasting fellowship of love to which we are called.

From Her Writings

'He loved me, He gave Himself for me' [Gal 2:20].
It seems to me that the whole doctrine of love,
which is true and strong,
is contained in those few words.
(L 252)

O Eternal Word…
I want to spend my life in listening to You…
that I may learn all from You.
Then, through all nights, all voids, all helplessness,
I want to gaze on You always
and remain in Your great light.
O my beloved Star, so fascinate me
that I may not withdraw from Your radiance.
(PT)

Give peace to my soul;
make it Your heaven,
Your beloved dwelling and Your resting place.
May I never leave You there alone.
(PT)

> *J. M + J. E.*
> *O mon Dieu Trinité que j'adore*
> *aidez moi à m'oublier entièrement*
> *pour m'établir en Vous immobile*
> *et paisible comme si déjà mon*
> *âme était dans l'éternité; que*

Heart to Heart

*I think that in Heaven my mission will be
to draw souls by helping them go out of themselves
to cling to God by a wholly simple
and loving movement,
and to keep them in this great silence within
that will allow God to communicate
Himself to them
and transform them into Himself.*
(L 335)

The Silence of the Heart

Once, while still a teenager, the future Elizabeth of the Trinity was asked by a family friend what she said to God during the long hours of prayer. *Oh, Madame*, she replied with disarming honesty, *we love each other.*[20] For Elizabeth, prayer was not a question of reason or logic: it was an affair of the heart, time spent apart with a Friend.

Every description of Elizabeth as a teenager portrays her as a bright, lively, intelligent young woman who loved music, hiking and travel. Yet at the same time, a deep spirituality and love of prayer were developing in her heart. In her personal notes of the period she writes: *May my*

life be a continual prayer, one long act of love. May nothing be able to distract me from you (IN 5). It is important to stress that, even as a teenager, Elizabeth was a contemplative in the world. She lived her Christian life in all its essentials without the support and structure of a religious community. She found her monastery in the *cell of [her] heart*, in that *little Bethany* (IN 5) where each heartbeat is an act of love. She wrote to a friend: *even in the midst of the world one can listen to Him in the silence of a heart that wants to belong only to Him!* (L 38).

Teacher of Prayer

Elizabeth can rightly be called a 'teacher of prayer', but not in the sense that she spells out for us a method or way of praying. Rather, she shares her own experience with us and invites us to open ourselves to the gift of the Spirit present in our heart. She challenges and encourages: *let us live with God as with a friend, let us make our faith a living faith in order to be in communion with Him through everything, for that is what makes saints* (L 122).

It would be wrong to think of Elizabeth as someone to be admired rather than imitated, a spiritual athlete rather than a fellow traveller. It is all too easy to visualise her as a gilded seraph, gliding through the corridors of prayer without a wayward thought or distraction! In her diary she humbly confesses her own struggle: *how hard and difficult prayer ordinarily seems. You have to work hard to gather all your powers together – how much it costs and how difficult it seems!* (D 14). Elizabeth was not above falling asleep in prayer or letting her attention wander. She confessed to her Prioress that sometimes she felt so dry and empty that she wanted to get up and run out of the chapel! On another occasion, she admits, she became so involved with her work of sewing that: *When I went to my prayer, try as I might, I could not rise above my 'rags'.*[21] For Elizabeth, no more than for the rest of us, rising above such 'rags' was not easy; she, too, had to struggle with her own restless thoughts and distractions.

Heart to Heart

Perhaps the phrase *heart to heart* best sums up the dynamics of Elizabeth's prayer: *I pour out my heart [to Him], I catch myself saying all sorts of foolish things…but He likes me to be uninhibited and to speak to Him heart to heart* (D 135). 'Heart', in this sense, represents the deepest part of her being, the centre of all her affections and love: *if you got to know Him a little, prayer wouldn't bore you any more*, she tells a young friend; *to me it seems to be rest, relaxation. We come quite simply to the One we love, stay close to Him like a little child in the arms of its mother, and we let our heart go* (L 123).

Elizabeth did not see her Carmelite life as irrelevant to her family and friends outside the convent. During her life in Carmel she wrote numerous letters; the majority of them were to lay people, with whom she shared the fruit of her own struggles. She tried to encourage and support them in whatever way she could. Her suggestions for rising above the 'rags' of distraction are as practical as they are sensible. Her constant plea is for simplicity: *when I say prayer, I don't mean so much imposing on yourself a lot of vocal prayers to be recited every day as that elevation of the soul toward God through all things* (L 252).

Look, Listen

Use whatever is helpful, she tells her friends: a book, favourite passages from scripture, rosary beads, a picture or a crucifix. To her mother she suggests *three prayers, five minutes each* (L 273), nothing long or complicated. Her advice to her sister Guite, who would soon be a young wife and mother, holds a universal lesson for all travel-weary pilgrims: *I would advise you to simplify all your reading, to fill yourself a little less, you will see that this is much better. Take your Crucifix, look, listen... don't be troubled when you are occupied like you are now and can't do all your exercises: you can pray to*

Elizabeth at the age of 13

God while working, it's enough to think of Him (L 93).

Prayer is not a matter of nice words or fine sentiments; it is a love affair of the heart: *there is no need for beautiful thoughts, only an outpouring of your heart* (L 273). Words are not the only vehicle of prayer: silence and listening are equally important. Above all, her advice is not to live on the surface but to find God *right in the depths, in the Heaven of [the] soul* (L 62): *You must build a little cell within your soul as I do. Remember that God is there and enter it from time to time* (L 123).

Open to Him

For Elizabeth, prayer was essentially a relationship – a friendship that must be reciprocated. *He wants to be the Friend you can always find. He is standing at the door of your heart... He is waiting... Open to Him* (L 174). Opening the door of the heart is the beginning of prayer. Discovering God's love for ourselves personally is an essential part of the journey of prayer. Elizabeth recommends brief moments of remembering the presence of God. It does not matter how we do this as long as we make the effort: *If you'd prefer to think that God is close to you rather than within you, follow your attraction, as long as you live with Him* (L 273).

When Elizabeth speaks of the prayer of presence, she is not speaking about feelings or of having a good memory. She is speaking about faith, attentive faith enlivened by love. It means awareness and attentiveness: finding God in the ordinary, everyday events of life. She says, *everything lies in the intention: how we can sanctify the smallest things, transform the most ordinary actions of life into divine actions!* (L 309). When she was in the kitchen, she admits that she did not go into ecstasy like St Teresa of Avila; she simply tried to be aware that the Lord was there with her, amid the pots and the pans (cf. L 235). It was the same experience in the laundry: *you see*, she explains, *...we find God at the wash just as at prayer* (L 89).

In the end, Elizabeth understood that all prayer is a sharing in the prayer of Christ: *Since Our Lord dwells in our souls, His prayer belongs to us, and I wish to live in communion with it unceasingly* (L 191). Prayer is entering into his heart, a heart of love. This is the reason for the silence and the listening, the attentive heart and the quiet mind. *I'm never alone: my Christ is always there praying in me, and I pray with Him* (L 123). Our prayer becomes his – and we pray with the heart of the Son to the heart of the Father.

From Her Writings

It is so simple to love,
it is surrendering yourself
to all His desires.
(L 288)

Remain in Me,
not for a few moments,
a few hours which must pass away,
but 'remain…' permanently, habitually.
Remain in Me, pray in Me,
adore in Me, love in Me,
suffer in Me, work and act in Me.
(HF 3)

It seems to me that if I saw death,
even despite all my infidelities,
I would abandon myself into the arms of my God
like a child who falls asleep
on its mother's heart.
(L 263)

Let Yourself Be Loved

You will never be commonplace
if you are vigilant in love!
But in the hours when you feel
only oppression and lassitude,
you will please Him even more
if you faithfully believe that He is still working,
that He is loving you just the same, and even more:
because His love is free
and that is how He wants to be magnified in you;
and you will let yourself be loved.
(LL 6)

Knowing We Are Loved

Every saint is a lover. Elizabeth of the Trinity was no exception. Her life was a constant search, inspired by the words of the apostle Paul, *to live through love in his presence* (Eph 1:4). To love, and to be loved, is the deepest of all human needs; it alone gives meaning and a sense of fulfilment to our lives. A few days before her death, Elizabeth said to her sisters, *Everything passes!... in the evening of life love alone remains...*[22]

The first and the greatest of all the commandments is to love God with every fibre of our being.

Yet, in a strange way, this presupposes something even more fundamental: to know how much we ourselves are loved. Love is a two-way relationship, a giving and receiving. It is the awareness of being loved that gives us our sense of worth and uniqueness; it helps us to  realise that we are special, and awakens within us our sense of individuality.

During the last days of October 1906, just two weeks before she died, Elizabeth wrote a 'farewell' note to her Prioress. Mother Germaine opened the letter after Elizabeth's death and never showed it to anyone. Its contents were revealed only in 1934, after Mother Germaine's own death. How often, over the years, she must have pondered on those precious words written from the heart of a daughter to her *Dearly loved Mother* (LL3).

Uncommonly Loved

There was a special bond of love and friendship between the Prioress and the young Elizabeth. In the letter, Elizabeth tries to convey her gratitude and appreciation for everything her Prioress has done for her; it is a deep and tender expression of love and affection. But Elizabeth was aware that Mother Germaine herself was diffident and apprehensive, often overwhelmed with the burden of responsibility. *You are uncommonly loved...*, Elizabeth tells Mother Germaine. *[Jesus] does not say to you as to Peter: 'Do you love Me more than these?'* Rather, his invitation is: *Let yourself be loved* (LL 2) – a phrase she here uses six times.

Thus, with great sensitivity and insight, Elizabeth reinterprets the words of the gospel to reassure Mother Germaine how greatly she is loved. The real invitation, Elizabeth insists, is for her to receive love, to open her heart to the gift of Jesus' love for her, without fear or apprehension: *let yourself be loved more than the others*, she writes, adding, *that explains everything...* (LL 3).

His Dream of Love

Elizabeth's words to Mother Germaine were an expression of her own spirituality, something she herself had discovered and that had become one of the principal sources of inspiration in her life. Fear had no part in Elizabeth's understanding of God: she knew herself to be a cherished daughter of her beloved Father. *It is love that makes His burden so light and His yoke so sweet*, she once said (L 220). It was a message she shared with others. As she wrote to a family friend: *if you knew how He loves you, how at every passing*

*moment He wants to give Himself to you more! I
am praying very much to Him, that He may carry
out fully the dream of His love in you* (L 241).

Words of Destiny

Elizabeth loved the scriptures and found in them a
constant source of inspiration and understanding.
She did not read widely: her reflection was more in
depth than in breadth. She pondered and savoured
her favourite passages, especially those from the
gospel of John and from her beloved Paul, *the
father of my soul.*[23] Two texts from St Paul were
pivotal in her understanding of her vocation –
'words of destiny', as they have been called:[24]

*Blessed be God the Father of our Lord Jesus Christ,
who has blessed us with all the spiritual blessings
of heaven in Christ.*
(Eph 1:3)

*They are the ones he chose specially long ago
and intended to become true images of his Son.*
(Rm 8:29)

In these words, Elizabeth discovered the immense
love of God, poured out in the gift of his Son.
And in Jesus we are called to become the Father's
beloved sons and daughters, sharing a life of
friendship and intimacy with God.

Elizabeth's cell – Dijon Carmel

This, Elizabeth believed – and she longed to share her insight with others – was a vocation not only for cloistered nuns, but for all the baptised called to share the joy and glory of being children of God through Jesus Christ. In Elizabeth's vision, there are no 'second-class citizens'. There is simply an invitation to all, to accept the gift of grace freely given in the Beloved. Once we discover this love, everything becomes different. She writes passionately to a young friend: *I understand that you need an ideal, something that will draw you out of yourself and raise you to greater heights. But you see, there is only One; it is He, the Only Truth!... He fascinates, He sweeps you away; under His gaze the horizon becomes so beautiful, so vast, so luminous... Since you need to live beyond yourself, live in Him; it's so simple* (L 128).

God – the Joy of my Life

The question is often asked: what is Elizabeth's most important message to the modern world? Many suggestions have been made: prophet of the presence of God, saint of the indwelling, lay contemplative, praise of glory. Perhaps John Paul II comes closest to providing an answer when, in his homily at her beatification in November 1984, he spoke of her as *a brilliant witness to the joy of being rooted and grounded in love* (cf. Eph 3:17). *Your Presence is my Joy* is how Conrad De Meester, in the title of one of his books, sums up the life and teaching of Elizabeth.

Her message is essentially one of joy – a joy that springs from knowing that I am loved, not in some vague, uncertain way but with a love that is personal and without limit. This is a love that does not depend on anything I have done or not done, it is not something I have to merit or earn: it is a gift. *God is love* (1Jn 4:8.16): he loves us with an everlasting love, whether we are aware of it or not. If he did not love us, he would cease to be God! As God, he can only love with infinite tenderness and compassion: *I have called you by name, you are mine... I have carved you on the palms of my hands!* (Is 43:1; 49:16).

The Greatness of Our Vocation

In September 1906, a few weeks before she died, Elizabeth wrote to her lifelong friend, seven years her junior, Françoise de Sourdon. This long, beautiful letter has been aptly called *The Greatness of Our Vocation*, both because our calling is *great*, and because it is *our* vocation

 – the call of every Christian. Elizabeth refers to her letter as a 'journal', but it is really a kind of meditation, a reflection on the meaning of life and the gift of faith: *Nourish your soul on the great thoughts of faith which will reveal to you all its richness and the end for which God has created you!* (GV 11).

Elizabeth wants Françoise to be free – free to live life to the full. She is not afraid to challenge her young friend to forget herself and *[live] by faith in God's presence*; this, she assures her, is *the secret of happiness* (GV 4). And she writes: *if we would think more about the origin of our soul, things here below would seem so childish* (GV 3). *It seems to me*, she adds, *the soul that is aware of its greatness enters into that 'holy freedom of the children of God'* (GV 4; cf. Rm 8:21).

Essentially, it is the heart that matters – the love by which we live our lives: *We must become aware that God dwells within us and do everything with Him, then we are never commonplace, even when performing the most ordinary tasks* (GV 8). Among her closing words to Françoise – and to all who listen with an open heart – is an invitation to surrender to this gift of love: *Believe in His love, His exceeding love* (GV 11; cf. Eph 2:4). This, she assures us, is the truth: *Truth is so beautiful, the truth of love* (GV 11).

From Her Writings

It is so good to give when one loves,
and I love Him so much,
this God who is jealous of having me
all for Himself.
I feel so much love over my soul,
it is like an Ocean I immerse and lose myself in:
it is my vision on earth while waiting
for the face-to-face vision in light.
He is in me, I am in Him.
I have only to love Him, to let myself be loved,
all the time, through all things:
to wake in Love, to move in Love, to sleep in Love,
my soul in His Soul, my heart in His Heart,
my eyes in His eyes, so that through His contact
He may purify me, free me from my misery.
(L 177)

For the Liturgy

Notes for a Homily

- Elizabeth of the Trinity speaks with a *prophetic force* (John Paul II). Her life has become a beacon of light, a call to discover once again the truth that God not only loves each of us personally but is uniquely and intimately present to us. At the heart of her teaching is the need for stillness and silence, a listening heart, open to hear the *still, small voice* of the Spirit within.

- Elizabeth's special grace seems to have been an awareness of the indwelling of the Trinity in her own heart and in the heart of all the baptised. By baptism we are called to enter into a deep and personal relationship with God; we become beloved daughters and sons of the Father, brothers and sisters 'in Christ', and the dwelling place of the Holy Spirit.

- Elizabeth did not speak of the Trinity in a logical or systematic way. For her the Trinity was not a dry, abstract truth; it was something to be lived and explored in the context of the 'good news' of the gospel. Jesus himself never used the word 'Trinity' but spoke of the special love and relationship between the Father and the Son, who together would send the gift of the Spirit into the hearts of all who believe.

- Elizabeth can be called a 'teacher of prayer', a witness to the reality and importance of prayer in our lives. She shares her own experience with us and invites us to open ourselves to the gift of the Spirit present in our hearts. She often found prayer difficult, was not above falling asleep at prayer or letting her attention wander. For her, prayer is not a matter of nice words and fine sentiments. It is a heart-to-heart sharing with a Friend. It is an awareness, enlivened by faith; an attentiveness to the present moment, learning to find God in all things – in the kitchen, at the wash, in the garden.

- The essential core of Elizabeth's message is that God is a God of love. She is *a brilliant witness to the joy of being rooted and grounded in love* (John Paul II). This is a love that does not depend on anything I have done or not done, it is not something I merit or earn. She liked to quote the words of St Paul describing God not just as loving but loving *to excess* (Eph 2:4). The whole focus of our lives is to receive this gift of love: *Let yourself be loved,* she says. *Believe in His love, His exceeding love... Truth is so beautiful, the truth of love* (LL 2; GV 11).

• Elizabeth found in Mary – *Gate of Heaven,* as she called her – one who fulfilled all her dreams and longings of being transformed into the image of Christ. For her Mary was mother, friend, companion and sister. The only one who has any impact in the world of grace is the one who, like Mary, is united to the heart of Christ. Elizabeth understood Mary's mission as being not only to lead us to her Son, but to help transform us into his image and likeness: *'The Virgin kept all these things in her heart': her whole history can be summed up in these few words! It was within her heart that she lived* (LR 40).

Prayers of the Faithful

As we celebrate the life and witness of Blessed Elizabeth of the Trinity, we turn to God in confidence for our needs and those of our community.

1. We give thanks to God the Father of our Lord Jesus Christ who has blessed us in Christ with every spiritual grace and blessing; may the

Church, the bride of Christ, grow ever more fully into his image and likeness.
Lord, hear us.

2. We give thanks for the gift of baptism we have received, by which we have become God's beloved sons and daughters; may we bear witness to this grace in our daily lives.
Lord, hear us.

3. We ask the Lord to deepen within us a love of prayer and to give us a spirit of stillness and silence, open to the gentle voice of the Spirit speaking in our hearts.
Lord, hear us.

4. May Mary, Mother of the Incarnate Word, deepen our love for her Son and teach us to follow him more fully along the way of the gospel.
Lord, hear us.

5. We pray for the Carmelite family and for all Christians throughout the world; may we be continually strengthened and renewed through the prayers and example of Blessed Elizabeth so that we may become, like her, a Praise of Glory.
Lord, hear us.

Father, we ask you, through the intercession of Blessed Elizabeth of the Trinity, to renew within us a deep spirit of faith and love, that we may become living witnesses of your presence in the world.

Prayer to Elizabeth of the Trinity

O Blessed Elizabeth,
teach us to live in faith and love
with the Holy Trinity
in the depths of our heart.
Teach us, like you,
to radiate the love of God
among men and women
in our daily living
so that we may be a
Praise of God's Glory.

References

1. For abbreviations, see Recommended Books.
2. He made this point in the foreword to his *Two Sisters in the Spirit: Thérèse of Lisieux and Elizabeth of the Trinity*, San Francisco: Ignatius Press, 1992, p. 11.
3. Words from John Paul II in his homily at her beatification; cf. Eph 3:17. The homily can be found in Conrad De Meester, OCD, 'Elizabeth in the Words of the Pope: "A New Guide – Certain and Sure"', *Mount Carmel*, vol. 55/2, 2007, pp. 16-20.
4. Conrad De Meester, OCD, *Your Presence is my Joy!: Life and Message of Blessed Elizabeth of the Trinity*, Darlington Carmel, n.d., p. 49.
5. This was the meaning given to Elizabeth, although the true meaning of her name comes from the Hebrew words 'Eli sheir', which signify 'God has sworn [made a promise / an oath]': see James McCaffrey, OCD, *Captive Flames: A Biblical Reading of the Carmelite Saints*, Dublin: Veritas, 2005, p. 127, note 39.
6. De Meester, *Your Presence, op. cit.*, p. 80.
7. *Ibid.*, p. 85.
8. See Recommended Books.

9. From the homily he gave at her beatification: see De Meester, 'Elizabeth in the Words of the Pope', *op. cit.*, p. 19.

10. In Jennifer Moorcroft, *He is My Heaven: The Life of Elizabeth of the Trinity*, Washington, DC: ICS Publications, 2001, p. 48.

11. See note 5.

12. Elizabeth is consciously quoting Thérèse of Lisieux who had addressed her own sister Céline with these words.

13. Pierre Barthez, 'Élisabeth Catez: une vraie musicienne!', in Jean Clapier, OCD (dir.), *Élisabeth de la Trinité: L'aventure mystique – sources, expérience théologale, rayonnement*, Toulouse: Éditions du Carmel, 2006, p. 573.

14. From *Elizabeth of the Trinity: Boundless Love*, a DVD produced by the Carmel of Dijon, 2006.

15. Office for the Promotion of Causes (ed.), *Elizabeth Still Speaks… – in the Processes of Beatification and Canonization: Words of the Servant of God Reported by Witnesses*, Eugene, OR: Carmel of Maria Regina, 1982, p. 7.

16. Barthez, *op. cit.*, pp. 568-9.

17. The first phrase is from Elizabeth's friend Marie-Louise Maurel, in *Elizabeth of the Trinity: Boundless Love, op. cit.* The second comes from her Prioress, in: [Mother Germaine de Saint-Seine], *The 'Praise of*

Glory': *Reminiscences of Sister Elizabeth of the Trinity – A Carmelite Nun of Dijon, 1901-1906*, London: R & T Washbourne, 1913, p. 7. While this translation has: 'Her soul, full of harmony' (a description by the biographer), Mother Germaine writes literally, in the French original: 'soul full of harmonies'. See also the excellent article: Jennifer Holden, 'Elizabeth the Musician: A Soul Full of Harmonies', *Mount Carmel*, vol. 55/2, 2007, pp. 9-15.

18. Office for the Promotion of Causes (ed.), *op. cit.*, p. 13.
19. In the title of the book by Hans Urs von Balthasar: see note 2.
20. Office for the Promotion of Causes (ed.), *op. cit.*, p. 7.
21. In Jean Lafrance, *Elizabeth of the Trinity: The Charism of her Prayer*, Darlington Carmel, [c.1983], p. 38.
22. De Meester, *Your Presence, op. cit.*, p. 84.
23. See L 240, note 4.
24. von Balthasar, *op. cit.*, p. 386.

Recommended Books

Elizabeth's Writings

So far, only two of the three volumes of Elizabeth's works have appeared in English (published by ICS Publications, Washington, DC). They cover her **writings and letters from Carmel** (and correspond to the French volumes I/a and I/b):

Vol. I   *Major Spiritual Writings* (1984)
Vol. II   *Letters from Carmel* (1995)

The works in these volumes are abbreviated in this book as:

HF   *Heaven in Faith*
GV   *The Greatness of Our Vocation*
LR   *Last Retreat*
LL   *Let Yourself Be Loved*
PT   *Prayer to the Trinity*
L   *Letters from Carmel [L 84-342]*

Writings from Elizabeth's youth, which will eventually become the third English volume, are translated here from the original (French volume II):

Œuvres complètes d'Élisabeth de la Trinité, vol. II, Paris: Cerf, 1985:

D   *Diary*
IN   *Intimate Notes*
L   *Letters from her Youth [L 1-83]*
P   *Poems*

Some of Elizabeth's **poetry** is already in English:

Alan Bancroft (tr.), *Barb of Fire: Twenty Poems of Blessed Elizabeth of the Trinity – with selected passages from Blessed Columba Marmion*, Leominster: Gracewing, 2001.

Elizabeth's Spoken Words

Office for the Promotion of Causes (ed.), *Elizabeth Still Speaks… – in the Processes of Beatification and Canonization: Words of the Servant of God Reported by Witnesses*, Eugene, OR: Carmel of Maria Regina, 1982.

Biographies

Conrad De Meester, OCD, *Your Presence is my Joy!: Life and Message of Blessed Elizabeth of the Trinity*, Darlington Carmel, n.d.

Jennifer Moorcroft, *He is My Heaven: The Life of Elizabeth of the Trinity*, Washington, DC: ICS Publications, 2001.

[Mother Germaine de Saint-Seine], *The 'Praise of Glory': Reminiscences of Sister Elizabeth of the Trinity – A Carmelite Nun of Dijon, 1901-1906*, London: R & T Washbourne, 1913.

Studies

Hans Urs von Balthasar, *Two Sisters in the Spirit: Thérèse of Lisieux and Elizabeth of the Trinity*, San Francisco: Ignatius Press, 1992.

Luigi Borriello, OCD, *Spiritual Doctrine of Blessed Elizabeth of the Trinity: Apostolic Contemplative*, Staten Island, NY: Alba House, 1986.

Jean Lafrance, *Elizabeth of the Trinity: The Charism of her Prayer*, Darlington Carmel, [c.1983].

----- *Learning to Pray: According to Sister Elizabeth of the Trinity*, Sherbrooke, QC: Médiaspaul, 2003.

Thomas Larkin, OCD, *Sister Elizabeth of the Trinity: A Carmelite Nun of Dijon 1901-1906 – An Introduction to her Life and Spirituality*, Dublin: Carmelite Centre of Spirituality, 1984.

M M Philipon, OP, *The Spiritual Doctrine of Elizabeth of the Trinity*, Washington, DC: Teresian Charism Press, 1947 (available in a reprint).

Shirley Darcus Sullivan, *Transformed by Love: The Soul's Journey to God in Teresa of Avila, Mother Aloysius of the Blessed Sacrament and Elizabeth of the Trinity*, Hyde Park, NY: New City Press, 2002.

Issues of Mount Carmel Magazine – Centenary 2006-2007

'Elizabeth of the Trinity – Centenary Issue', *Mount Carmel*, vol. 54/3, 2006.

'Elizabeth of the Trinity – End of Centenary Issue', *Mount Carmel*, vol. 55/2, 2007.

CDs and DVDs

Eugene McCaffrey, OCD, *Blessed Elizabeth of the Trinity*, Carmelite Monastery, Kirkintilloch – set of 4 CDs.

Donna Orsuto & James McCaffrey, OCD, *Discovering Bl. Elizabeth of the Trinity: A Carmelite for Today*, Carmelite Forum (recorded by Éist, Dublin), [2005] – set of 2 CDs or cassettes.

Carmel of Dijon, *Elizabeth of the Trinity: Boundless Love*, Dijon: Carmel of Dijon, 2006 – 1 DVD (jointly in French, English & German).

Carmel of Dijon & Massimo Manservigi, *Sabeth: Élisabeth de la Trinité 1880-1906*, Dijon: Carmel of Dijon, 2006 – set of 3 DVDs (jointly in French, English, Italian & Spanish or: French, English, German & Polish).

Some Forthcoming Titles from the Teresian Press

A Moment of Prayer – A Life of Prayer
  – Conrad De Meester, OCD

What Carmel Means to Me
  – Edited by James McCaffrey, OCD
  & Joanne Mosley

John of the Cross: Seasons of Prayer
  Iain Matthew, OCD

How Do I Pray Today?
  – Edited by James McCaffrey, OCD
  & Joanne Mosley

Upon this Mountain:
Prayer in the Carmelite Tradition
  – Mary McCormack, OCD